C 523.45 LAN

WITHDRAWN
Landau, Elaine.
Jupiter /
MOSQ 1079715920

WORN SOILED. OBSOLETE

D0603425

A TRUE BOOK™

Jupiter

ELAINE LANDAU

Children's Press®
A Division of Scholastic Inc.
New York   Toronto   London   Auckland   Sydney
Mexico City   New Delhi   Hong Kong
Danbury, Connecticut

Content Consultant

Michelle Yehling

Astronomy Education Consultant

Aurora, Illinois

Reading Consultant

Linda Cornwell

Literacy Consultant

Carmel, Indiana

Library of Congress Cataloging-in-Publication Data

Landau, Elaine.
Jupiter / by Elaine Landau.
    p. cm.—(A true book)
Includes bibliographical references and index.
ISBN-13: 978-0-531-12559-5 (lib. bdg.)   978-0-531-14789-4 (pbk.)
ISBN-10: 0-531-12559-9 (lib. bdg.)   0-531-14789-4 (pbk.)
1. Jupiter (Planet)—Juvenile literature. I. Title. II. Series.
QB661.L36 2008
523.45—dc22   2007003869

No part of this publication may be reproduced in whole or in part, or stored in a retrieval system, or transmitted in any form or by any means, electronic, mechanical, photocopying, recording, or otherwise, without written permission of the publisher. For information regarding permission, write to Scholastic Inc., 557 Broadway, New York, NY 10012.

© 2008 Elaine Landau.

All rights reserved. Published in 2008 by Children's Press, an imprint of Scholastic Inc.
Published simultaneously in Canada. Printed in China.
SCHOLASTIC, CHILDREN'S PRESS, A TRUE BOOK, and associated logos are trademarks and/or registered trademarks of Scholastic Inc.
2 3 4 5 6 7 8 9 10 R 17 16 15 14 13 12 11 10 09 08   62

Find the Truth!

Everything you are about to read is true *except* for one of the sentences on this page.

Which one is **TRUE**?

T or F   Jupiter has rings around it.

T or F   Space probes have brought back samples of Jupiter's rocks and soil.

Find the answer in this book.

Contents

THE **BIG** TRUTH!

Earth

A space shuttle carried the *Galileo* spacecraft into space.

The spacecraft *Galileo* orbited Jupiter for more than eight years!

4 A Stormy Planet
Just how long can one storm last? **27**

5 Rings and Many Moons
How is a planet like a whole solar system? . . . **32**

6 Missions to the King of the Planets
Has anything entered Jupiter's dangerous atmosphere? **39**

This is a copy of a telescope made about 400 years ago by a scientist named Galileo.

5

Jupiter

Saturn

Mars

Venus

It is unusual to see five
planets in the night sky.
The planets line up like
this once every 20 years
or so.

Mercury

CHAPTER 1

A Trip to Jupiter

Jupiter is the third-brightest object in the night sky, after the moon and Venus.

Jupiter has fascinated people since early times. The ancient Romans named the planet after their most powerful god. Romans believed that the god Jupiter ruled the heavens. In one way, the planet Jupiter also rules the heavens. Jupiter is bigger than all the other planets in our **solar system** combined!

The Roman god Jupiter was the brother of Neptune and the son of Saturn.

Pioneer 10 **took this photograph in 1973.**
Pioneer 10 **was the first spacecraft to visit Jupiter.**

Imagine that you could travel to Jupiter. Jupiter is the fifth planet from the sun. Earth is the third planet from the sun. So, blasting off from Earth, you would travel away from the sun. As you flew closer to Jupiter, you would see a beautiful planet covered with orange, brown, and white stripes.

Jupiter's stripes are really layers of frozen clouds. The clouds are different colors because they're made of different types of gas and ice.

Jupiter looks beautiful. But you wouldn't want to get too close to it. The storms on Jupiter are bigger and fiercer than any storms on Earth.

Do you think the name Jupiter fits this huge, stormy planet? Read on to learn more.

Jupiter has a storm that's bigger than Earth!

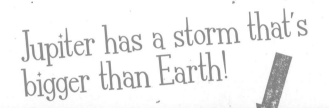

This giant storm "eats" smaller storms that get too close.

An artist created this illustration of Jupiter and Earth to show the difference in the planets' sizes.

CHAPTER 2

Jupiter in the Solar System

Jupiter is so big that more than 11 Earths would fit across it.

Jupiter is one of eight planets in our solar system. The other planets are Mercury, Venus, Earth, Mars, Saturn, Uranus, and Neptune. All of these planets **orbit,** or circle around, the sun. Together, these planets have at least 162 moons. The solar system also has many icy **comets** and rocky **asteroids**.

Jupiter's Solar System

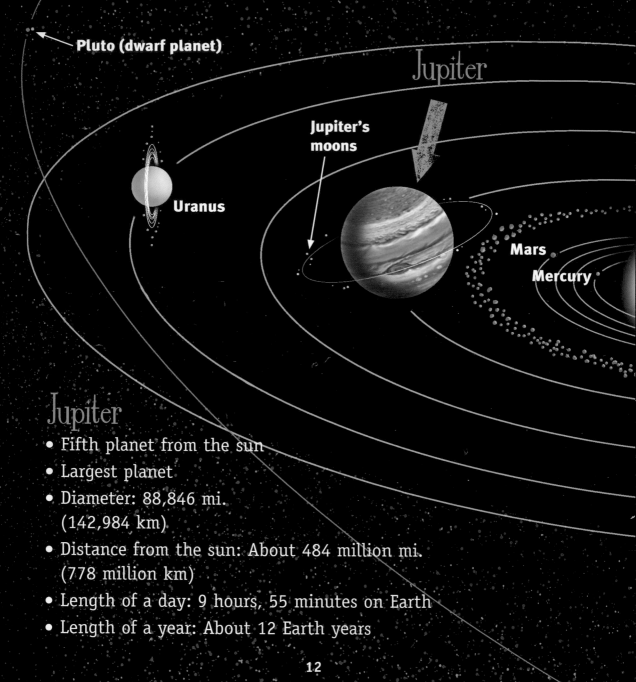

Pluto (dwarf planet)

Jupiter

Jupiter's moons

Uranus

Mars

Mercury

Jupiter

- Fifth planet from the sun
- Largest planet
- Diameter: 88,846 mi. (142,984 km)
- Distance from the sun: About 484 million mi. (778 million km)
- Length of a day: 9 hours, 55 minutes on Earth
- Length of a year: About 12 Earth years

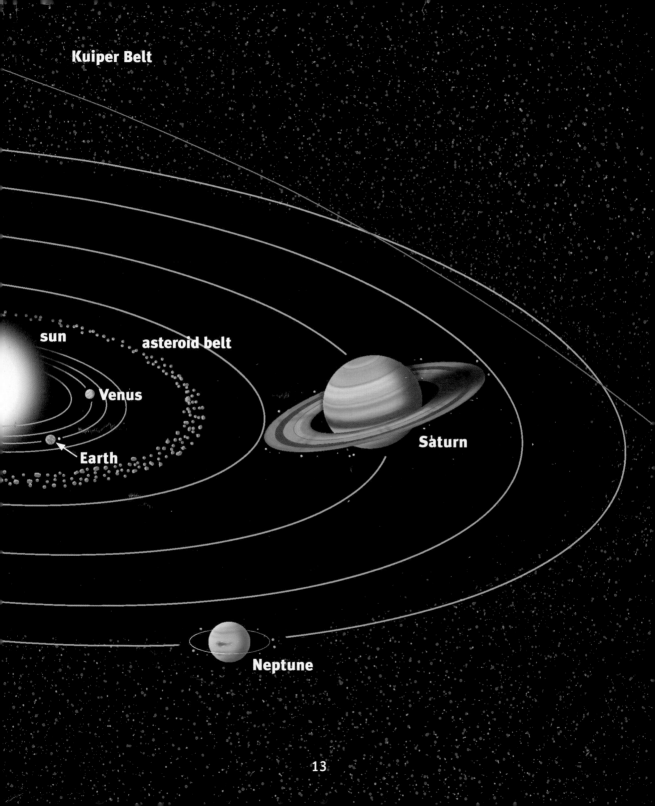

Kuiper Belt

sun

asteroid belt

Venus

Earth

Saturn

Neptune

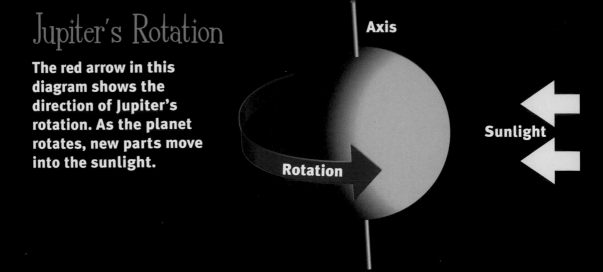

The red arrow in this diagram shows the direction of Jupiter's rotation. As the planet rotates, new parts move into the sunlight.

Axis

Sunlight

Rotation

A Day on Jupiter

As Jupiter orbits the sun, it also **rotates**, or spins, on its **axis**. An axis is an imaginary line that runs from north to south through the center of a planet.

The amount of time it takes a planet to rotate once on its axis equals one day on that planet. Jupiter completes one rotation in about 9 hours, 55 minutes. So Jupiter's day is less than half as long as a day on Earth. It's really spinning!

This illustration shows what Jupiter might look like from space. Behind it are the sun and other stars. In reality, the sun would appear smaller than it looks here.

Jupiter is 5 times farther from the sun than Earth is.

These illustrations of Jupiter were created on a computer. They show Jupiter's rotation. Can you follow the red spot as it moves in the top row of photos?

A Year on Jupiter

The time it takes a planet to orbit the sun once equals one year on that planet. One year on Jupiter is almost as long as 12 years on Earth. Why?

Jupiter is much farther from the sun than Earth is. So Jupiter has to travel farther than Earth to complete one orbit. It takes Earth a little more than 365 days to complete its orbit around the sun. But it takes Jupiter almost 4,331 Earth days to orbit the sun. That equals almost 12 Earth years.

How Old Are You Now?

You celebrate your birthday once a year. Each planet has a year of a different length. A year on Jupiter is much longer than a year on Earth. How old would you be on Jupiter and other planets?

If you are 10 years old on Earth, you would be:

Planet	Age
Jupiter	10 months old
Mars	5 years old
Venus	16 years old
Mercury	41 years old

This is an artist's vision of what Jupiter's upper atmosphere looks like.

CHAPTER 3

What's It Like on Jupiter?

A spaceship trying to land on Jupiter would sink right into the planet!

It would take a spaceship more than a year to travel to Jupiter. But the journey would be the easy part. A spaceship would have a hard time getting through Jupiter's thick **atmosphere**, or the blanket of gases that surrounds a planet or moon. What's more, the ship would find no solid surface to land on!

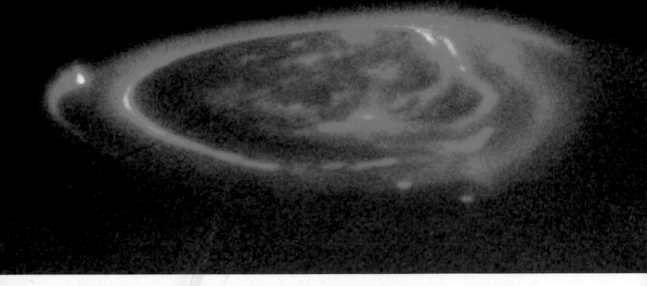

There are rings of glowing gas around Jupiter's poles, or ends. Here you see the glow around Jupiter's north pole.

Any spaceship passing through Jupiter's clouds would be squeezed by the tremendous pressure of Jupiter's atmosphere. Every planet with an atmosphere has this **atmospheric pressure**. You don't notice it on Earth because it is just the right amount of pressure for life on this planet. You could not survive without Earth's pressure pushing on you. Jupiter's pressure is too great for a human body to survive.

Gas Giant

Jupiter has no solid surface. The planet is made mostly of gas and liquid. If you tried to stand on Jupiter, you would sink into an ocean of gases!

Jupiter is not the only planet that's a **gas giant**. Saturn, Uranus, and Neptune are also giant balls of gas and liquid.

Jupiter is made mostly of **chemicals** that can also be found on Earth. But you would not be able to breathe on Jupiter. Jupiter has very little oxygen. People and animals need oxygen to breathe.

The pressure of Jupiter's atmosphere would crush a spaceship.

Under the Clouds

Jupiter is mostly made of a chemical called hydrogen. In the atmosphere, the hydrogen is a gas. This changes inside the planet. The deeper into the planet you go, the greater the pressure. Hydrogen gets squeezed by this pressure until it becomes a liquid.

Pressure can also cause materials to heat up. Temperatures rise high inside of Jupiter. The deeper you go, the hotter it gets. The hottest part is Jupiter's core, or center. The temperature there may be as hot as 55,000 degrees Fahrenheit (30,000 degrees Celsius)!

The temperature in Jupiter's core may be five times higher than it is in Earth's core.

Jupiter's and Earth's Interiors

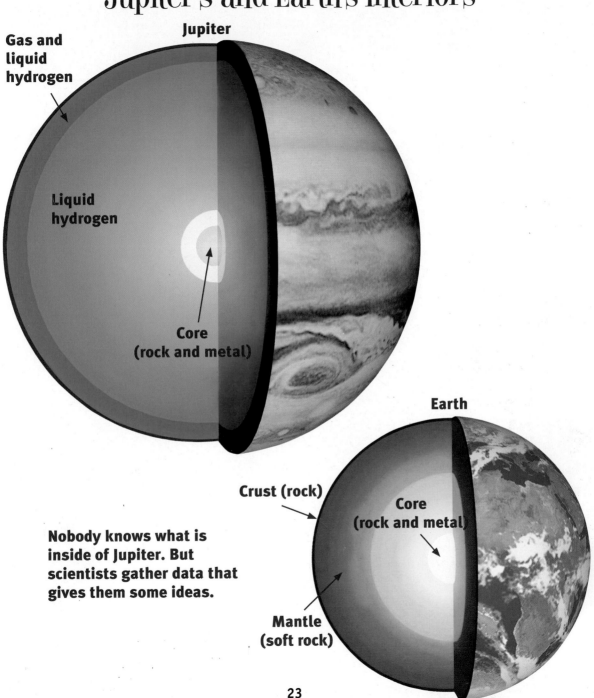

Jupiter

Gas and liquid hydrogen

Liquid hydrogen

Core (rock and metal)

Nobody knows what is inside of Jupiter. But scientists gather data that gives them some ideas.

Earth

Crust (rock)

Core (rock and metal)

Mantle (soft rock)

How Big Is Jupiter?

If Jupiter were the size of a soccer ball, then Earth would be the size of a marble! See how the other planets compare in size to Jupiter, the king of the planets.

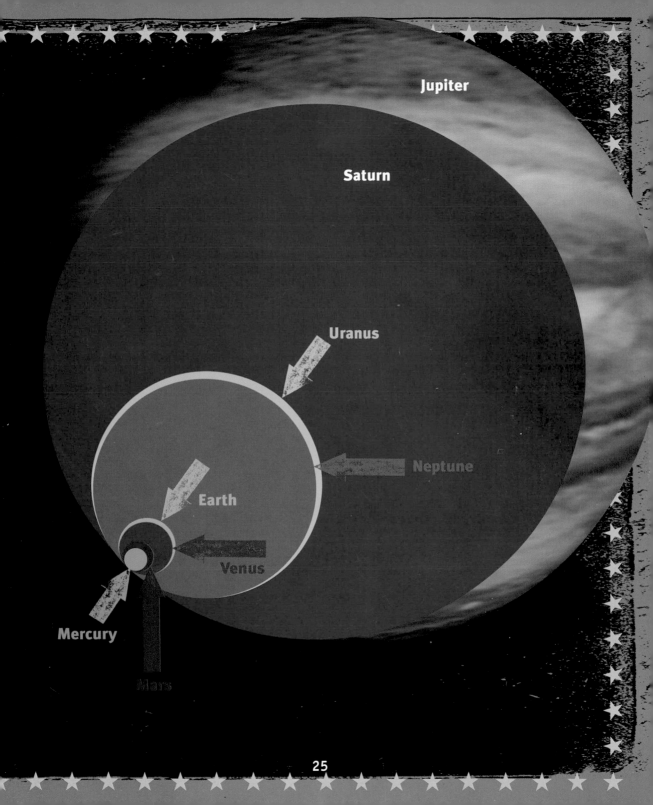

These images show part of Jupiter's atmosphere. The one on the left is true color. Scientists added the colors to the image on the right to show more clearly Jupiter's different types of clouds. Deep clouds are reddish, and high, thick clouds are white.

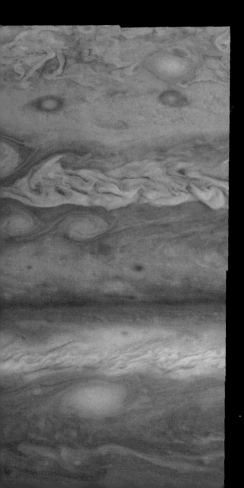
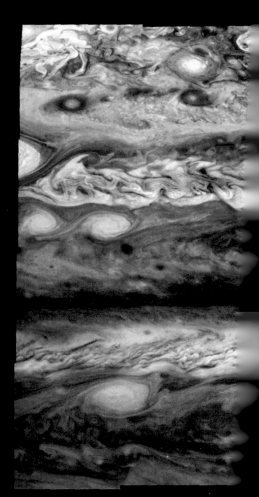

CHAPTER 4

A Stormy Planet

Storms on Jupiter can rage for hundreds of years!

Jupiter has thunderstorms, just like Earth. But its giant storms make Earth's biggest storms look tiny. Winds on Jupiter are much stronger than any winds on Earth. They blow in all directions. Giant lightning bolts crack, and thunder rumbles.

27

Storms on Earth begin with heat from the sun. The sun heats up areas of Earth's atmosphere. Hot air rises. When pockets of air rise, other air moves in to replace it. That's how wind is formed.

On Earth, winds blowing at more than 90 miles (145 kilometers) per hour bend trees and create large waves.

Huge frozen clouds float above the liquid layer of Jupiter. Scientists think the dark spot in this photo is a hole in the clouds.

Jupiter is far from the sun. It receives little of the sun's energy. In fact, the clouds you see on Jupiter are frozen. The temperature of the clouds is around −186°F (−121°C). But Jupiter has its own source of heat. Heat from Jupiter's interior rises into its atmosphere. This extreme heat creates tremendously strong winds.

Jupiter's quick rotation on its axis also makes the winds swirl very fast. Jupiter's winds can reach 400 miles (645 km) per hour. That's about twice as fast as Earth's strongest winds.

Red Spot

The most famous storm on Jupiter is called the Great Red Spot. This huge, oval-shaped storm is a mass of spinning clouds. The storm's winds whirl at about 250 miles (400 km) per hour. This storm might be more than 300 years old!

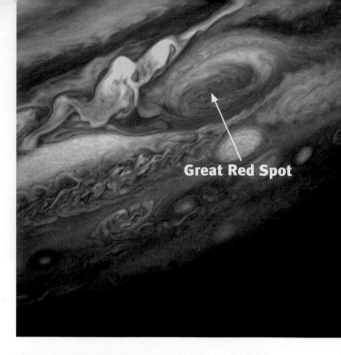

Great Red Spot

The Great Red Spot is half as large as it was 100 years ago.

The Great Red Spot is about 15,400 miles (24,800 km) in diameter. Nearly two Earths could fit inside it. That's one huge storm!

Little Red Spot

Another storm on Jupiter is nicknamed the Little Red Spot or Red Spot Junior. It has been a weaker storm than the Great Red Spot, but its winds are becoming more powerful.

There have been some interesting changes in this smaller storm. At the end of 2004, the Little Red Spot looked white in photographs taken from space. By 2006, it had turned a reddish color.

The Little Red Spot's color change surprised **astronomers**. They think the storm's winds may have swept up some red material from lower in Jupiter's atmosphere.

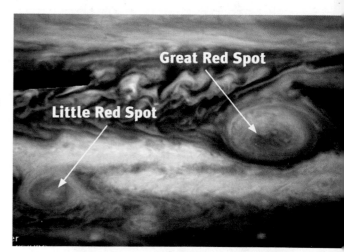

Great Red Spot

Little Red Spot

The Great and Little Red Spots might one day join together. The two storms pass close to each other every two years.

CHAPTER **5**

Rings and Many Moons

Jupiter has more moons than any other planet in our solar system.

Jupiter is part of Earth's solar system. But in a way, this planet is like the center of its own mini–solar system. Astronomers have discovered a ring system and 63 moons that orbit Jupiter. And there may be more rings and moons waiting to be discovered.

Io Europa

Io and Europa, two of Jupiter's moons, are approximately the size of Earth's moon.

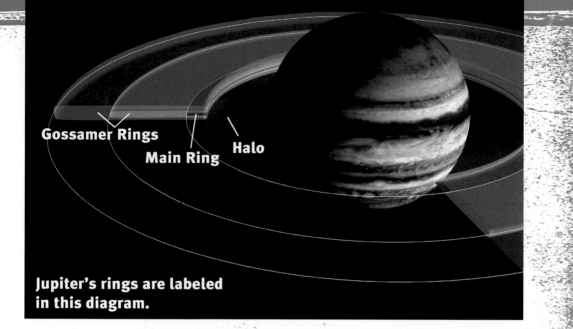

Gossamer Rings

Main Ring **Halo**

Jupiter's rings are labeled
in this diagram.

Jupiter's Rings

Jupiter's ring system has three parts. The outer part
is called the gossamer (GAHS-uh-mer) rings. There
are two gossamer rings. The brightest part in the
middle is called the main ring. Inside the main ring
is the third part, a ring called the halo.

Saturn's famous rings are made mostly of ice.
But Jupiter's rings are made up of dust and bits of
rock. How were these rings formed?

Four moons orbit inside of Jupiter's rings. Astronomers think that the rings were formed from parts of these moons. Asteroids and comets may have smashed into the moons. Particles flew off the moons during each crash and formed rings.

The layer of ice on a moon called Europa may be several miles thick!

Finding Jupiter's Large Moons

1610

Ganymede

Io

Callisto

Europa

34

Galilean Moons

Four of Jupiter's largest moons were first seen from Earth in 1610. They were discovered by the astronomer Galileo. So the moons are known as the Galilean (gal-uh-LAY-in) moons. Their names are Ganymede (GAN-uh-meed), Europa (yuhr-OH-puh), Io (EYE-oh), and Callisto (kuh-LIST-oh). The largest Galilean moon is a little bigger than Mercury. The smallest is about the size of Earth's moon.

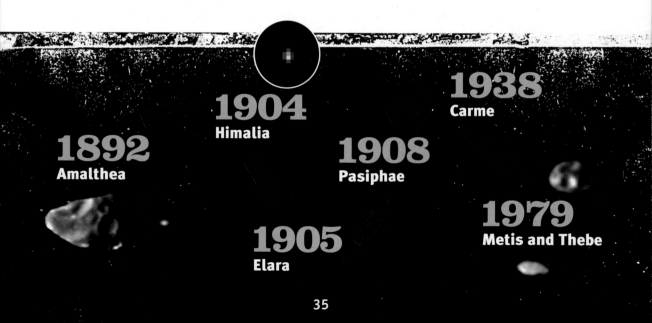

1892
Amalthea

1904
Himalia

1905
Elara

1908
Pasiphae

1938
Carme

1979
Metis and Thebe

Ganymede is the largest moon in the solar system. Ganymede is made of rock and ice.

Europa is the smallest of the four Galilean moons. It is a little smaller than Earth's moon. Europa's surface is mostly ice. Astronomers think there may be water or watery slush under the ice.

Io is the Galilean moon that is closest to Jupiter. Io has many active volcanoes. They are spewing hot lava as you read these words!

Callisto is the third-largest moon in the solar system. Its rocky surface is covered with holes called craters.

Io's volcanoes put out more heat than any other body in the solar system.

In 1979, *Voyager 2* captured this image of Volcano Loki erupting on Io.

Loki

The Wonders of a Telescope

The Italian astronomer Galileo spent hours studying the night sky. At first, he was limited to what he could see with just his eyes.

In 1609, Galileo learned that Dutch sailors used an instrument called a telescope. It made faraway objects appear closer. The sailors used it at sea to search for land.

Galileo built his own telescope. Using it, he spotted small specks of light near Jupiter. He had found four of Jupiter's moons. They later became known as the Galilean moons.

Galileo also used his homemade telescope to study the surface of Earth's moon.

This illustration shows a space probe released by *Galileo* into Jupiter's atmosphere. The cone at the bottom is a heat shield. It kept the probe from burning up as it entered the planet's atmosphere.

CHAPTER 6

Missions to the King of the Planets

A space probe fell into Jupiter's atmosphere at more than 100,000 mph.

People have been able to see Jupiter in the night sky for hundreds of years. But recently, space probes have been sent to explore Jupiter more closely. A space probe is a spacecraft that does not carry astronauts.

Pioneer 10 was the first space probe to travel near Jupiter. It gathered information from space for more than 30 years.

The first space probe to study Jupiter was launched in 1972. *Pioneer 10* took the first close-up pictures of Jupiter as it flew by the planet. In 1974, *Pioneer 11* took more pictures of Jupiter and its moons. *Voyager I* and *Voyager II* flew past Jupiter to gather information.

Voyager 2 was launched in 1977. It is expected to transmit data until approximately 2020.

An artist created this image of *Galileo* as it flew above Io on its way toward Jupiter.

In 1989, the *Galileo* spacecraft was launched. It was the only probe to orbit Jupiter. *Galileo* sent photos and information about the planet's temperature back to Earth. *Galileo* was the first spacecraft to observe a comet colliding with a planet. Its mission was supposed to last for two years. It kept working for eight years!

Galileo carried a smaller probe. The probe parachuted down into the dangerous atmosphere of Jupiter. It gathered information for an hour before it was crushed by the planet's strong pressure.

What's in Jupiter's Future?

Exciting new missions to Jupiter have been planned. In 2010, the *Jupiter Polar Orbiter (Juno)* may be launched. If it is, the **orbiter** will circle Jupiter's north and south **poles**. It will help us to learn more about the planet's size, temperature, and winds.

Then in 2015, Jupiter's moon Europa may be further explored by the *Europa Geophysical Explorer*. This spacecraft would study this moon's icy surface and the water beneath it. It would also look for possible landing sites for future missions.

As time passes, the king of the planets is becoming less mysterious. With more advanced space probes, the upcoming missions may be the most exciting of all. ★

One of the aims of the Juno mission is to find out how much water there is in Jupiter and its atmosphere.

True Statistics

Classification: Gas giant

Number of moons: At least 63

Diameter: 88,846 mi. (142,984 km)

Atmospheric temperature: −230°F (−145°C)

Distance from the sun: About 484 million mi. (778 million km)

Length of a day: About 9 hours, 55 minutes on Earth

Length of a year: About 12 Earth years

100-pound (45 kg) person would weigh: 236 lb. (107 kg)

Top wind speed in the Great Red Spot: 400 mph (644 kph)

Number of years this storm has been raging: More than 300

Did you find the truth?

T Jupiter has rings around it.

F Space probes have brought back samples of Jupiter's rocks and soil.

Resources

Books

Carson, Mary Kay. *Exploring the Solar System: A History with 22 Activities*. Chicago: Chicago Review Press, 2006.

Jackson, Ellen. *The Worlds Around Us: A Space Voyage*. Minneapolis: Millbrook Press, 2006.

Koppes, Steven N. *Killer Rocks from Outer Space: Asteroids, Comets, and Meteors*. New York: Carolrhoda, 2003.

Lassieur, Allison. *Astronauts*. Danbury, CT: Children's Press, 2000.

Panchyk, Richard. *Galileo for Kids: His Life and Ideas, 25 Activities*. Chicago: Chicago Review Press, 2005.

Somervill, Barbara A. *The History of Space Travel*. Mankato, MN: The Child's World, 2004.

Taylor-Butler, Christine. *Jupiter*. Danbury, CT: Children's Press, 2008.

Organizations and Web Sites

NASA's Solar System Exploration

www.solarsystem.nasa.gov/kids

Find fascinating information about the solar system.

National Space Society

www.nss.org

1620 I Street NW, Suite 615

Washington, DC 20006

202-429-1600

This organization works toward humans living and working in space.

Galileo Project

www.jpl.nasa.gov/galileo

Here you'll find great pictures of Jupiter!

Places to Visit

Kennedy Space Center

Kennedy Space Center, FL 32899

www.ksc.nasa.gov

Take a tour of KSC's giant rockets and launch pads.

Smithsonian National Air and Space Museum

Independence Avenue at 4th Street, SW

Washington, DC 20560

202-633-1000

www.nasm.si.edu

See the world's largest collection of historic airplanes and spaceships.

Important Words

asteroids (AS-tuh-roidz) – large pieces of rock that orbit the sun

astronomers (uh-STRAW-nuh-murz) – scientists who study the planets, stars, and space

atmosphere (AT-mu-sfihr) – the blanket of gases that surrounds a planet or other object

atmospheric pressure (AT-mu-sfihr-ik PRE-shur) – the force of the weight of gases in the atmosphere pressing down

axis (AK-siss) – an imaginary line that runs through the center of a planet or other object

chemicals (KE-mih-kuhlz) – substances or mixtures of substances

comets – large chunks of rock and ice that travel around the sun

gas giant – a planet made mostly of liquid and gas; Jupiter, Saturn, Uranus, and Neptune are gas giants

orbit – to travel around an object such as a sun or planet

orbiter – a spacecraft made to orbit an object without landing on its surface

poles – the areas at the very north and very south of a sphere

rotates – spins on an axis

solar system (SOH-lur SISS-tuhm) – a sun and all the objects that travel around it

Index

About the Author

Award-winning author Elaine Landau has a bachelor's degree from New York University and a master's degree in library and information science from Pratt Institute.

She has written more than 300 non-fiction books for children and young adults. Although Ms. Landau often writes on science topics, she especially likes writing about planets and space.

She lives in Miami, Florida, with her husband and son. The trio can often be spotted at the Miami Museum of Science and Space Transit Planetarium. You can visit Elaine Landau at her Web site: www.elainelandau.com.

PHOTOGRAPHS © 2008: age fotostock/Les Cunliffe: 24 left; AP Images/NASA: 34 right center; Bridgeman Art Library International Ltd., London/New York/Fitzwilliam Museum, University of Cambridge, UK: 4 top, 7; Corbis Images: 34 left center (NASA), 3, 9 (Roger Ressmeyer/NASA); Getty Images: 16 (William Radcliffe), cover, 15 (Antonio M. Rosario), back cover (Space Frontiers), 10 background (Mark Weiss/DigitalVision); NASA: 8, 34 left (Ames Research Center), 20 (John Clarke/University of Michigan), 31 (ESA/HubbleSite), 29, 30, 32, 40, 42 (JPL), 33, 35 left, 35 right (JPL/Cornell University), 34 right (JPL/German Aerospace Center), 21 (JPL/Space Science Institute), 34 center (JPL/University of Arizona), 36 (JPL/USGS), 41 (JSC), 26 (University of Arizona), 5 top, 39; Pat Rasch: 14, 12, 13; Photo Researchers, NY: 23 bottom, 23 top (Mark Garlick), 4 bottom, 10 foreground, 25, 27 (Victor Habbick Visions), 38 (David A. Hardy), 6 (Jerry Lodriguss), 18 (Shigemi Numazawa/Atlas Photo Bank), 28 (Jim Reed); Photodisc, Inc./C Square Studios: 24 right; Scholastic Library Publishing, Inc.: 44 top, 44 bottom; Superstock, Inc./age fotostock: 17; The Granger Collection, New York: 37 top; The Image Works/SSPL: 5 bottom, 37 bottom.